T0162314

The Essence of Spiritual Life

The Essence of Spiritual Life

a companion guide for the seeker

Swami Rama

Himalayan Institute Hospital Trust
Swami Rama Nagar, P.O. Doiwala,
Distt. Dehradun 248140, Uttaranchal, India

Originally published as *Sadhana: The Essence of Spiritual Life*.
©1996 by Swami Rama
©2002 by the Himalayan Institute Hospital Trust

First USA edition, 2002
Printed in the United States of America
ISBN 8-190100-49-1
Library of Congress Control Number 2002105137

Published by:

Himalayan Institute Hospital Trust
Swami Rama Nagar, P.O. Doiwala,
Distt. Dehradun 248140, Uttaranchal, India
Tel: 91-135-412068, Fax: 91-135-412008
hihtsrc@sancharnet.in; www.hihtindia.org

Distributed by:
Lotus Press
P.O. Box 325
Twin Lakes, WI 53181
www.lotuspress.com
lotuspress@lotuspress.com
800-824-6396

ALL RIGHTS RESERVED. No part of this book may be reproduced in any form or by any electronic or mechanical means including information storage and retrieval systems without permission in writing from the publisher, except by a reviewer who may quote brief passages in a review.

*My life is like a slate on which are drawn a few lines
by a great sage of the Himalayas,
and with a feeling of gratitude
all the petals of the flower of my life
are offered to him.*

Other books by Swami Rama

Sacred Journey:
Living Purposefully and Dying Gracefully

Conscious Living:
A Guidebook for Spiritual Transformation

Yoga the Sacred Science, volume one:
Samadhi The Highest State of Wisdom

Let the Bud of Life Bloom:
a guide to raising happy and healthy children

Contents

Foreword

Spiritual life is a wonderful life. If you are on the path, you are bound to commit mistakes and you are bound to stumble, simply because you are a human being. On the way, the mind goes through many confusions because life within and without are totally different.

One has to create a bridge between the two. A systematic method is essential for understanding the subtle levels of life within, and the changing patterns of the external world that is constantly subject to change, death, and decay.

Those who can serve as beacons are needed. No one person can effectively illuminate the way for everyone. There is more than one main road and a great number of subroads.

In the many years that we have been blessed by the presence of Swamiji, his teachings have served as cherished beacons of light, helping to illuminate every precarious step of crossing the bridge.

The Essence of Spiritual Life, is a gathering together of some of the brightest rays of those beacons, collected from Swamiji's lectures, notes, and letters written to aspiring students. The last section of the book, Reflections from the Silence, is comprised of excerpts from Swamiji's personal diary of his own experiences along the path.

This concise and condensed collection reflects the brilliance of the subtle essence of Swamiji's systematic teachings. Its light shines for all seekers of Truth who may need assistance along the way.

Dr. Rajesh

Introduction

One objective of the *sadhana* of all believers in God is to be somewhat godlike. As God's universe, which is both his garment and Self-expression, is not a dreary desert, the life and externals of a godlike person need not always be the imitation of a desert.

As bare deserts are, however, a phase of God's creation, asceticism may be a phase of God-seeking and Self-realization, but not the whole of it. Genuine asceticism for finding one's own soul and for the good of humanity is worthy of reverence.

Equally worthy of reverence, if not more, is the treading of the fuller and more difficult path of sadhana of those who are in the world, but remain above it.

The lotus is often used as a symbol in Indian culture and mythology because the lotus grows in the mud, yet remains above, untouched and unaffected by the mud and water.

You can live in the world and yet be spiritual. It is not necessary for you to renounce the world. Wherever you are, stay there. Simply follow two formulas. One formula is for living in the external world:

> All the things of the world that are given to me are given to me by the Lord. They are meant for me and I have the right to use them, but I don't have the right to possess them, for they are not mine.

All things will become means in life if you have this attitude, instead of, "This is mine, this is mine." You are afraid of losing what you have; you are afraid it will decay and go to decomposition. You should learn to use the things of the world without being possessive. As St. Bernard said, "Love the Lord alone. Use the things of the world as your means."

In addition, you should do your actions selflessly, lovingly, and skillfully.

Nothing more than that is needed—one formula for the external world.

What to do for the inner self?

> God is everywhere. The Lord is in me; I am his shrine. As a shrine is kept neat and clean, I will try my best to keep my body, breath, and mind pure and orderly.

For a person of wisdom who knows the Truth, internal and external are one and the same. Inner freedom is born of self-sacrifice, self-purification, and self-control. This freedom releases the spirit and gives it wings to soar to the boundless sphere of the unfathomable levels of being.

Freedom is truth. Why then do we live in a cage with no sky beyond it—in a closed world of hard facts? We are like seeds with hard outer coverings, crying from within for liberation. Millions of people die like seeds that have lost the urge for generation.

The resources for living and being successful on the earth that are offered by Mother Earth for her children are immense, but those who are not aware of the real and limitless resources lying dormant within human life are deprived, and this self-deprivation is the cause of suffering.

Shall there be a day when the consciousness of the large multitude will be illumined? Only then will human beings and society understand the profound meaning of the Reality that offers us love and emancipation.

The joys received through prayer, meditation, and contemplation are the highest of all joys. I am one living witness who confirms that the highest of joys cannot be given by the world. All the joys in the world give you but a taste. That taste can never be satisfied. A momentary joy is called *vishaya ananda*. It is *ananda* (bliss), but it lasts only for a short time.

Sages say there is another ananda—*paramananda*—that is something higher, something everlasting, something that can never be snatched, and that is liberating and emancipating.

What is unique in the human being is the awareness of consciousness. The burning desire to attain immortality, the perfect, and the eternal, makes the human being superior to all other creatures.

Sadhana is prescribed for the attainment of a happy life on the earth, in heaven thereafter, and at length, liberation. Spiritual practices lead the aspirant toward divinity or inner experiences that further help to attain the final goal of life.

Entire life is sadhana.

You ask, "Is it possible for me to know God? Is it possible for me to be a spiritual person? Is it possible for me to do this?"

Patanjali, the codifier of yoga science, says, "O aspirant, learn to practice until the last breath of your life."

Let the heavens shower all the blessings upon you, so that you can grow and unfold yourself, and accomplish the purpose of life. My prayers are always with you.

With all my love and blessings.

Swami Rama

Truth

Truth is that Divine Force that dwells in every individual's heart. It is the all-pervading, eternal Reality, uniting all individuals, and finally, linking all of existence in one divine awareness. That Divine Force is called God.

Belief in the existence of God indicates that one is searching for the Truth. The Truth is that which remains unchanged in the past, present, and future. The Truth is unborn and immortal. To know Truth, one needs to purify one's thoughts, speech and actions. Purification is of utmost importance, because only through a purified mind can an aspirant think clearly and contemplate.

Once we are determined to search for the Truth through purified thoughts, speech, and actions, we are certain to find the way and reach the goal. Truth itself becomes our guide, and without making a mistake we will find ourselves on the right path.

One who believes in God and surrenders to God attains freedom here and now. He knows that he belongs to God, and that God belongs to him. His awareness shifts from the world to God, and he lives a life free from insecurity and fear. He has an unshakable faith in divine protection.

The scriptures constantly remind us that as the ocean accepts a river and makes it its own, God accepts seekers. It does not matter which path they follow or from which background they come. The only requirement is the desire to know the Truth. Once that desire is awakened, all means and resources come together. Water finds its own level. Likewise, a true lover of God finds God.

The highest philosophy is to know that the Truth and God are one and the same, and the highest practice is to search for Truth through one's thoughts, speech, and actions.

There is something beyond religion. Though essential in the preliminary stage, it does not allow one to be one with the whole. It is like a moth that eats Kashmir wool, trying to prove to other moths that Kashmir exists. Everywhere in the realm of religion I encountered locked doors. If ever one door should chance to open, I was ultimately disappointed by what lay behind it.

God's existence does not depend on our proofs. There is something wrong with the philosophers and the theologians, for they have the curious notion that God is a kind of hypothesis that can be analyzed and discussed.

I have seen people struggling with death because they do not admit its existence. God to me is a real annihilating fire and indescribable grace. I accept both.

It is easy to believe in God, and to believe in God is definitely better than not believing, however, that is only half way. It is something great when you come to know that:

> God is in me. The Lord dwells in me. I am a finite vessel, and Infinity dwells within this finite vessel.

The human being is great, not because he can speak and narrate things, and not because he can feel. He is great because wherever he goes, the Lord travels with him.

No one has seen God. Highest of all, love without object, is God. How to know him? How to enjoy?

Seeing God in everyone and working for others is one way of enjoyment, but that is not so easy. You will have to practice. Remember the Lord all the time and sooner or later, you will be transformed.

The day you come to know that the Lord is within you, you will be free from fears. Then where are you? Where do you exist? If you have that consciousness that you exist separately from the Lord of the Universe, then it means you deny the existence of the Lord of the Universe.

God is all—a personal God, a universal God, and that which is beyond. Start from a personal God, go to the God within, then to the universal God, and finally beyond.

To love beloved God in any object is knowledge, yet to understand God in the heart is real Truth. It is a vain attempt to search for God. Who can there be more wonderful than myself—that is the Self of all.

Those who crave to see God are foolish. When I see him smiling through the face of man and child, and highest of all in myself, I am born a million times, and die a million times, too.

No God is greater than thyself.

The Goal

Human birth is not an accidental phenomenon, it has a purpose. A human being is born to accomplish a goal.

In life everything does not happen the way you want it to happen, therefore, patience and determination are two virtues that, if properly nurtured and cultivated, can lead one to attain the goal. The goal is to meet God face to face, and then live in the world and yet remain above, unaffected.

Every human being is born with all the means and resources necessary to attain the goal. Human beings should know how to use their resources efficiently and skillfully. The power of thought is the highest tool by which one can decide what ought to be done and what ought to be avoided. Through the power of thought, one tries to know the purpose of life and the means to achieve it. He wonders about who he is, from where he has come, and ultimately, where he will go. The power of thought does not allow him to rest until he has unveiled all the mysteries of life.

The highest mystery that a human being wants to unveil is to know the nature of thinking itself, the source from which the thinking process originates, and ultimately, the true nature of one's own Self.

The stream of life may change its course. It may shift from one state to another, it may become manifest or unmanifest, but it never stops. It keeps flowing until it merges and becomes one with the ocean, the pure Supreme Consciousness.

Floating in the eternal stream of life, a human being has gone through innumerable life states. The stream of life is filled with experiences of, and reactions to, one's countless births and deaths. Death and birth seem to be an unending cycle.

The only way to get out of that cycle is to accept the superiority of discrimination, willpower, and divine inspiration over sensory perceptions and cognition. One must change one's worldview and start looking at life from a higher perspective.

One should break this cycle systematically, step by step. First, one should realize the nature of the transitory objects of the world, and the amount of satisfaction derived from them. The objects of the senses are a source of joy as long as they are not in hand. Once they are attained, the senses and the mind soon become dissatisfied and search for other objects.

The knowledge about worldly objects and the tendency of the senses and the mind helps the seeker to change his perception. A feeling of dispassion arises in the heart. Knowledge born of dispassion inspires one to change the course of one's life and begin exploring the possibility of finding eternal peace and happiness.

Spiritual desire consumes all trivial desires and attachments. The power of discrimination becomes active. One performs one's actions with full discrimination. He purifies his thoughts, speech, and actions, and as a result of that purity, one day he receives divine illumination from above.

The Path

The path of Truth is narrower than the needle's eye and as sharp as a razor's edge.

When you start expanding your consciousness, you will come to know that on the path of spirituality there is always guidance from the unknown. We have come from the unknown and we will return to the unknown. We remain in the known for only a short time, but the unknown is always with us. Therefore, we should rely on the unknown. If we are treading the path of light, and if by chance, by mistake, by ignorance, or even by bad habit, we commit mistakes, we will return to the path again, because of the guidance from the unknown.

When you study you will find many paths and many ways and methods. All roads lead to only one goal. If you practice and learn to follow one path for a few days, and after some time follow another path, and then after a month follow another one, that is not going to help you.

When you are searching and seeking, you should be doing it honestly with your full strength—not halfheartedly.

If your dearest one stands in the way of Self-realization, tread over him, forsake him, go beyond. If your beloved stands in the way of Self-realization, cast her aside. Your trusted friend is Truth and Truth alone.

O Lord, make me not stumble on the path of Truth.

The Architect

When a human being learns to seek religion not in gods, but in his own potentials, then he will know that he is great and that within his greatness lies his happiness. When he rapidly unfolds the chapters of life's manuscript, of which he himself is the author, he begins to realize who he is.

You are the architect of your life. You build your own philosophy and construct your own attitudes. Without right attitudes, the entire architecture remains shaky. Once you realize this fact, you will look within.

Once you turn your focus inward, the process of transformation will begin, and naturally you will become aware of many levels of consciousness. You will find that the capacity to know yourself is within, and this realization will become a source of fulfillment to you. The sages in the past have experienced this fact, and have documented their experiences.

Unfortunately, people in the modern era do not know how to benefit from the wisdom of the sages. As a result, people are still searching for happiness in the external world.

If you study life's journey, when you start unfolding yourself and experiencing life and its necessities, you will find throughout that life is full of changes and modifications. Let you learn to enjoy life from moment to moment and do not worry about the future. If you take care of your present, the future will be at your disposal, and one day you will find out that you are the architect of your life.

Spirituality

It is not necessary to retire to a monastery to lead a spiritual life. We cannot escape from our inherent longings or postpone our utmost needs. In addition to the primitive urges for food, sex, sleep, and self-preservation, there is a higher urge to merge with God. We cannot be at peace unless that inherent divine urge is fulfilled.

We all want to experience the all-pervading, omnipresent God from which the entire universe, as well as each individual, has evolved. Direct experience of the truth that each of us originates from God, and ultimately will return to God, makes us secure, happy, and strong.

Today millions of educated men and women are suffering from a lack of purpose. Lacking also in self-confidence, young girls and boys have become victims of dissatisfaction and frustration. Along with a worldly education, we must provide some spiritual education.

Human beings have done research on three levels so far on mind, energy, and matter. Yet we have not found out a way to live in peace, to attain happiness that is free from all problems, pains, and miseries. We study this "ism," and that "ism." We go to this church and that temple. We seek advice from this swami and that other yogi. Yet, we have not found the way.

The whole confusion lies in the fact that we do not understand ourselves, and yet we introduce ourselves to others.

We are strangers to ourselves yet we get married, have children, have homes, and claim to love others.

That training that helps us to attain a state of happiness free from pains and miseries, is missing from our daily life. Nobody teaches us how to look within, how to find within, how to verify within.

We are taught to know and see things in the external world, but this inner training and knowledge is missing. When we graduate with flying colors from colleges and universities, we find that we are still unsatisfied. The big questions about life still remain questions:

> Who am I? From where have I come? What is the purpose of life? Where will I go from here?

Modern education helps us to understand and to be successful in the external world, the world of means. It doesn't help us to know ourselves.

To know yourself, you don't have to go anywhere. If you want to know yourself, you have to follow the path from the grossest to the subtle, then to the subtler, and finally, to the subtlest aspects of your life. You have to search for yourself, because religions do not fulfill this need.

I am not telling you not to follow your religion, or not to believe and trust in your religion. Often religions do not answer certain vital questions of life. Religions tell you what to do and what not to do, but religions do not tell you how to be.

No matter how many temples and churches we build, nothing is going to happen unless we accept one principle—

that the greatest of all churches and temples is the living human being.

The scriptures say:

> The greatest of shrines is the human body. Look within and find within. There His Majesty dwells in the inner recesses, in the inner chamber of your being.

The day you come to know this, you will be happy. To believe in God is not a bad thing. It is a very good thing, because at least you have faith; but you should not forget that God is within you.

As a part of our educational training, we must define spirituality in its most precise and universal terms. Spirituality means that which helps us discipline our thoughts, speech, and actions, that which leads us toward the center of consciousness, and thereby unfolds our inner potentials.

Education based on such spiritual guidelines will help humanity to become self-reliant, confident, and active in the external world. At the same time, it will enable humanity to broaden its world view, and to become inward to search for the perennial Truth. Only a spiritually based education can bring harmonious balance to our external and inner lives.

Knowledge of theories that prove the existence of God is not as important as learning to discipline oneself, so that God can be experienced directly. Children should be taught how to sit quietly and make their minds one-pointed. Through their calm and one-pointed minds, children can obtain a glimpse of true peace and happiness. We need not force them to believe that there is a God; however, we should provide them with the opportunity to unfold their inner potentials, gain confidence, and become inspired to search for God, according to their own inner tendencies and backgrounds. Children need to cultivate divine virtues within themselves.

That which is purely physical has its limits, like the shell of an egg. Spirituality has infinite horizons and limitless freedom. It is full of knowledge and perennial light, life, and delight. When one is completely detached, one realizes oneself in a wider and deeper relationship with the Universal Being.

When ego becomes aware of something that is higher than ego—the individual spirit, or soul—then spirituality dawns.

Spirituality dawns when individuality vanishes.

Sadhana

Sadhana is important. It will give you a comprehensive knowledge of life with all its currents and crosscurrents.

It is amazing to observe that most of the people enveloped in sloth and lethargy are not aware that life on this earth is but a brief moment, and that moment should be utilized to purify the way of the soul. Those who do not do their duties and yet expect the best in life, are fools who live in a fool's paradise.

In life's primitive paradise, fools aspire to live for a long time. They live perpetually on charity. They are beggars who are burdens to society and even to themselves. These beggars are envious of one another and habitually suspicious of each other, like dogs living upon their master's favors, showing their teeth, growling, barking, and trying to chew up one another. Their very existence is described as a struggle. Their paradise lacks peace, equilibrium, and tranquility.

I worked hard in my life and attained something that gives me solace. I found out that life is mingled with sorrow and joy; both of these feelings should not be allowed to disturb the course of life.

A human being is not imperfect, but incomplete. Man's essential nature is a limitless horizon. The call to inner Truth is present in him with all profundity, but his analytical logic is shallow.

Peace cannot be attained through mere speculative philosophy or logic. I am willing to believe that philosophy is useful for the comprehension of the Ultimate Reality, but I do not admit that philosophy alone can lead us to the ultimate goal. However great the philosophy may be, it must be supplemented by faith, emotion, and strict discipline of the functions of the will.

A *sadhaka* has to go through a series of internal experiences. When a sadhaka's convictions are filtered by the systematic and organized way of sadhana, the mind becomes penetrating and one-pointed.

An aspirant must control the dissipation of the mind. Conquest over the senses and the mind helps one to attain freedom from the charms and temptations of the world. Free from worldly distractions, nothing remains in the mind but the longing to know God.

Once such an exclusive longing awakens, one becomes absorbed in contemplating and meditating on God. Through constant contemplation and meditation, one begins having glimpses of the Truth, and these experiences strengthen his faith. Growing internally, that exclusive faith becomes the source of inner strength, enabling the aspirant to move along the path until perfection is achieved.

The first detachment achieved by the aspirant is physical, inspiring him to develop the power of instinctive love and knowledge that helps him to relate with the world and nature. Nature has her own laws and helps all creatures to receive her blessings and grace in many ways.

The human mind is complex with all its typical moods, manners, and weapons. The purpose of sadhana is to be free from the magic wonders of the mind and remain free all the time.

Freedom is a divine gift lent to mortals. A seeker of Truth should first have freedom from all time-honoured taboos. Mental freedom is an accepted fact and is definitely higher than physical freedom. Free spirit is godly and alone can claim kinship with God.

The potential to realize the Truth is present in every person. In some it remains dormant, while in others it is awakened. The more one directs one's awareness toward the Divine Force, the more one realizes the emptiness of the objects of the world. That realization helps one to withdraw one's mind from the external world, and to compose oneself for inner exploration.

All sadhanas, all practices, are meant to purify and strengthen the mind that disturbs your being and prevents you from being aware of the Reality that is within you.

To be spiritual means to be aware of the Reality all the time, to be aware of the Absolute Truth all the time, and to be aware of the Lord within you all the time.

Citizen of Two Worlds

Lacking in foresight, people consider their present condition and circumstances alone to be the truth. Taking their present condition for granted, they refuse to explore the possibility of other states of existence. The conscious part of mind fails to grasp that which lies beyond the spheres of time, space, and causation.

There is a more illumined part of human beings that is aware, at least subliminally, that reality is more than what is known and seen. According to the scriptures, the unmanifest, and therefore unseen and unknown, aspect of reality is higher than the manifest world.

That which takes place in the physical world is a mere reflection of what has already taken place in the inner world. The nature of inner life changes the quality of external life. The way we think forms our personality.

Without proper thinking and discrimination, a human being fails to see his essential oneness with the Truth and, therefore, identifies with the external garment, the body. False identification with the body makes one a victim of pain and pleasure. Insatiable desire for pleasure and aversion to pain force one to keep transmigrating from one life to another.

A human being is a citizen of two worlds, and he or she has to develop the ability to have access to both without any confusion. Clarity of mind comes if you have learned to direct your mind according to your desire and goal.

The world within and the world without are two entirely separate realities. The external world dissipates energy, but the internal world showers blessings that fill the vacuum created by the world.

Conquering the inner world is more difficult than succeeding in the kingdom of life in the external world. One journeys from one success to another failure, for one is not trained to travel into the subtler levels of life.

When awareness expands, it expands on two dimensions simultaneously: one toward the internal Self, where there is peace, happiness, and bliss; the other toward the external world that is full of profusion and confusion.

The inner world is governed by the more subtle force of the Divine. Spirituality means allowing the inner world to remain illumined by the light of the Divine Force. The thoughts, speech, and actions of an illumined person are in perfect harmony. Such a person knows he is a citizen of two worlds simultaneously.

Have a balance between the internal and the external worlds. Do not be caught by the rigidity of external observances, which are actually nonessentials. Do not be affected by the suggestions of others, but learn to follow your own way that does not hurt, harm, or injure anyone.

Outsiders suffer a lot, but insiders can attain emancipation and enlightenment. Fortunate few are those who successfully create a bridge between the two realms, within and without.

Self - Transformation

For a genuine and everlasting transformation, one must practice a systematic method of self-discipline and self-training. Mere philosophy and intellectual knowledge cannot stand in time of need, if one does not know how to use the essentials of that philosophy in one's daily life. Applying theoretical knowledge and living with it in daily life is called practice.

Practice requires discipline. Discipline should not be rigidly imposed, but students should learn to commit themselves and accept discipline as essential for self-growth. Imposing rigidity and following it is not helpful at all.

On the way to self-transformation, self-discipline is indispensable to both those who live in the world and those who renounce the world and resort to monasteries. Even those who renounce their homes and duties still carry with them the deep-rooted *samskaras* sown in earlier lives. It takes a long time to become free of those samskaras.

Becoming a swami or monk is not so important. What is important is to accept a self-disciplined life. There needs to be a bridge between life within and without. Discipline is the foundation of that bridge. People should not be tempted by mere techniques, but should learn to cultivate discipline within themselves.

People have formed a habit of leaning on others. They always want others to help and tell them what to do and what not to do. This is a bad habit. You are a human being; you should take charge of yourself. If you become too dependant on a therapist, a preacher, or a healer, then what's the difference between you and an animal? It means you are allowing your life to be governed by your trainer. By becoming dependent on such therapies and therapists, your power of self-motivation and self-guidance will never be allowed to unfold. The scriptures, the treasure house of the sages' experiences, clearly state that self-help alone helps. For such self-help we need a sound method of self-training.

Among all the methods for training and therapies, the highest of all is self-training in which one remains conscious of one's thoughts, speech, and actions. When you work with yourself you will notice that whenever you calm down your conscious mind, bubbles of thoughts will suddenly come up from the unconscious mind.

In learning to control the mind and its modifications, it is essential to go through the process of self-observation, self-analysis, and meditation. Learning to control the mind, and careful study of the relationship between the conscious mind and the unconscious mind, take a long time. Many times you may think that you have conquered your thoughts and your mind is under your control. After a few days, some unknown bubble arises from the unconscious and disturbs your conscious mind, thus changing your attitudes and behavior.

The process of transformation requires regularity and vigilance. Without regularity it is not possible to transcend one's habit patterns or transform one's personality. Patience helps one maintain regularity, whereas self-analysis and observation help one remain vigilant.

At times you may find yourself disappointed and depressed, but if you are determined and committed to self-training and self-transformation, you will certainly find help in one way or another. Do not worry about success, failure is a part of success. However, not to make an effort is wrong.

The kicks and blows and constant battles that I had to go through, I alone know. I am giving you loving advice and I hope you follow it with full determination.

Inner Strength

If something does not turn favorable in life, one should learn to forget and start a fresh chapter. Strength, strength, strength is a necessity for leading a happy life and that strength should be inner strength.

Learn to be strong from within.

When you learn to live on inner strength, you emanate that inner strength, and that will help others too.

Where is the Lord? The Lord is within you, seated deep beyond your mind and emotions. You should say the God-centered prayer:

> I am Thine and Thou art mine. I need strength, please give me strength. In any situation I'm in Lord, give me strength.

One day you will have so much inner strength that you will witness the Reality, the absolute Truth within, and then you will be happy.

Fearlessness

Fears, if not examined, will develop strong roots, though they are often rootless. Fear invites danger.

Self-preservation is the instinct that remains always vigilant to protect the body. This instinct is useful up to a certain extent, but it should not become an obsession in life. When fear becomes an obsession, all spiritual potentials become dormant. Fears are never examined—that is why they are able to control human life. They should be examined boldly.

Fear has two faces: I might lose what I have, and I might not gain what I want. These two thoughts should not be entertained, and cannot be when you remember your mantra or the presence of the Lord within.

Fearlessness is very important. One should constantly remain in spiritual delight, so that no fear is entertained. Fearlessness comes from knowing that God is with us, and that we are with God.

Faith

Faith based on direct experience bestows the clarity of mind that is necessary for functioning in the world of objects, and for penetrating into the many unknown levels of life. Such faith can never be challenged, whereas blind faith is always subject to scrutiny.

Belief in God, and experiencing the presence of God at every moment, are two different things. Before the actual direct experience of the Truth, one may believe in the existence of God, but that belief remains imperfect.

True belief, which is known as faith, comes after direct experience. Faith born from direct experience becomes a part of the aspirant's being, and such faith protects the aspirant like a mother protects her child.

A belief established on the solid foundation of the Truth is a source of strength. A belief based on the direct experience of the Truth, and not contradicted by logic and reasoning, is known as *shraddha*, or faith.

Such faith is established over an extended period of time. Repeated experiences add to the maturity of the faith. Direct experience of the Truth removes all doubts and leads an aspirant to a decisive understanding. Such an understanding becomes an inseparable part of his being. Knowledge becomes firm and he does not feel it necessary to seek verification from others. He knows that he knows. Such is his faith.

On the basis of that faith, he starts his quest and reaches his goal. Belief in God may lead one to a series of disappointments. Faith in God leads one to God.

Determination

Faith and determination are two essential rungs on the ladder of enlightenment. Without them enlightenment can never be realized. Without faith we can attain some degree of intellectual knowledge, but only with faith can we see into the most subtle chambers of our being.

Determination is the power that sees us through all frustrations and obstacles. It helps in building the willpower that is the very basis of success within and without. It is said in the scriptures that with the help of *sankalpa shakti*, the power of determination, nothing is impossible.

Shakti is behind all the great works done by the great leaders of the world. When the power of determination is not interrupted, one inevitably attains the desired goal.

Decide that no matter what happens, you will do what you set out to do. If you are determined, possible distractions will still be there, but you will continue on your path and remain undisturbed.

Sankalpa (determination) is very important. You cannot change your circumstances, the world, or society to suit you. If you have strength and determination, you can go through the procession of life very successfully.

Be confident, self-reliant, and always say to yourself, "I will do it. I can do it. I have to do it." These confirmations build the power of determination, or sankalpa shakti.

Patience

In sadhana patience plays an important role.

Patience is a great virtue that needs to be cultivated. One should always pay attention to one's determination, sincere efforts, patience, regularity, and loving nature. Always try to be vigilant, so that the opposite forces do not take over.

Whenever you find an obstacle, you should learn to be patient. You will have to be patient when you go to the unconscious mind, to the many fields of your mind.

The mind says, "How come you are so brave to go to the kingdom of the Lord within, without dealing with me?" Sometimes it becomes a devil; sometimes it becomes an angel; sometimes it becomes evil; sometimes it becomes a sage. It has all these qualities. The mind is a means for bondage—it could be a means for liberation. If the mind is at your disposal, it will not create obstacles for you.

You should learn to be patient. The quest of the soul helps you, if you persist; then, finally, you will find the light from the distance that dispels the darkness of ignorance. Will you please practice?

The time will come when you will know all that is to be known. Do not allow the gentle and eternal flame to diminish, and do not give name to the nameless.

Self-Condemnation

There is no need to condemn yourself by thinking, "I am bad, I am bad, I cannot do anything." You waste so much time in condemning yourself. Who are you to condemn yourself? You don't belong to yourself. Your body is made of five elements. You cannot create the body again, so your body does not belong to you. Your *pranas* do not belong to you; your mind does not belong to you; your soul does not belong to you. Who are you to claim that this is bad and that is good? Both claims are not helpful. One feeds the ego, the other cripples your creativity.

Do not condemn yourself. You have no right to do that. You are created by Providence and you should learn to respect its creation. When you stumble against yourself you will also stumble in the external world. Don't hurt yourself. Be strong.

How come you are picking up the habit of having an inferiority complex? It means you feel you are a lump of flesh, a bag of bones, and a tumbler of blood with a mechanical brain inside your skull. You are more than that. You are a luminous soul, a spark of the eternal fire of Atman. You are the way you think and you become the way you think. Stop having that inferiority complex. What you eat, do, and think is limited to the body, breath, and mind.

The Buddhist scriptures say that if you hate others, nothing happens to the hated person, something happens to you, to your mind, to your heart. You can learn to love somebody, even one whom you hate, by understanding that he is a human being like you. Who am I to hate that person? Stop hurting and hating others, for it injures you. If you constantly injure yourself, it can lead you to an action that can never be forgiven by your own mind, by your own conscience. You are constantly killing your conscience. Stop doing that.

The Ishopanishad tells you not to kill your conscience. When you kill your conscience, how can you love others? You should learn to appreciate, admire, and love yourself, and then emanate that love to others.

If someone else injures you it can be treated, but if you go on injuring yourself, who will treat you? The greatest sinner is he or she who constantly kills his or her own conscience. The Upanishads declare it.

Remember that fifty percent is my job and fifty percent is your job. I do my job and you do yours. Suppose you don't do your job; I will still continue my efforts to help you grow.

A human being commits many mistakes because he is not perfect. When you sit down in meditation, have a little dialogue with yourself. What did I do today that was not right? What did I say that was injurious and harmful? This way of keeping track of ideas, thoughts, action, and speech is called housekeeping.

A human being is like a multistoried mansion. In this mansion there are many subtle and finer forces of life. To manage such a magnificent mansion, you have to supervise all the levels of the mansion, not only the primitive fountains of food, sex, sleep, and self-preservation.

Those who are ignorant get lost in gross objects that are subject to change, death, and decay. They are not aware of the finer forces of life that are the real interior functionaries of this mansion of life. Body is only a gross tool. Breath is finer, and finest is the mind.

Actions are actions, and you should not identify yourself with your actions. You should learn to build a personal philosophy and remain free from any guilt.

When you have a dialogue with yourself and find that you have committed a mistake, do not repeat it. Why brood on mistakes and create a deeper feeling of guilt for yourself?

If actions that you consider to be injurious or obstacles to the path are not repeated, then you are free. A guilt feeling comes because you are creating a law for yourself, or society is creating laws for you. If you follow the law of life, there is no reason for you to have a guilt feeling.

You are your own judge, but don't be obsessed by don'ts. Life was not meant for don'ts. The more you make your life calm, the more it becomes purified, and the whole philosophy changes. This is a process of self-transformation that actually helps you to grow, unfold, and attain.

Those who know all about their mind and its various aspects, enjoy and attain the beauty of life. Life should be appreciated. No one has the right to condemn it.

What is good and what is right, thinking makes it so. Surrender the mind for a while to God consciousness, and you will find peace.

Forgiveness

People constantly identify themselves with their thought patterns. Thoughts are virtually actions. To identify yourself with actions is not good. To be caught by the blind rules and injunctions of society is to create a prison for yourself.

You should not brood on past actions. That which has been done, is done. If you want to do it again, do it again. To allow your mind to travel to past grooves creates a bad habit that in time becomes part of your life.

You should learn to forgive yourself. Those who do not forgive themselves never forgive others. Forgiveness is the greatest of all virtues.

Beauty

Express yourself with all the gentleness that you can, for gentleness and love are one and the same. If you learn this lesson, you can transform many lives. How beautiful is that life that knows not the ugliness of abrupt and rough behavior.

The most beautiful person is she who is always filled with joy and moves in that joy. Such movements make one a great dancer. Learn to practice this dance.

If you go to the end of the earth and search for yourself, you will never meet anyone like you. You are the only one and there is none to compare with you. You are exceptionally, uniquely, one piece of art created by the greatest of all artists, the Divine.

Don't become a victim of the impositions forced upon you by this society that always robs the simplicity and profundity of the beautiful. Learn to appreciate your own beauty. A human being can never hide his or her ugliness by colorful clothes. The more simple you are the more beautiful you look. By God, you are beautiful, and there is none equivalent to your beautiful face.

Dharma

Learn to enjoy life and do not form the habit of worrying. There is nothing of mystery in life, but life has a shadow of its own. All individuals carry their shadow no matter where they go. This shadow is like a huge bag in which are contained a trillion ideas, desires, thoughts, and feelings. Poor human beings remain carrying that burden 'til the last breath of their lives.

In the course of fulfilling the above mentioned desires, people assume certain duties that are called *dharma*s. Every individual has a dharma, and that dharma should not have a clash with the collective dharma of the family in which he or she is born, nor with the society in which he or she lives.

Adjustment leads to contentment.

Happiness

Three things are important: first to learn to love your duty, and second, to have the concept that all the things of the world are means and are not meant to be possessed.

The third thing is to remember to be happy in all situations. No matter where you go, in any situation, whatever you do, morning, afternoon, and night—learn to be happy. Never forget that!

Whatever people consider happiness to be is a concept and varies according to age and experience. Many people are content, whether they have something or not. Others are never content, no matter how much they have.

Happiness is not what you want, but wanting what you have.

In some villages in India, they still use a method of drawing water from a kind of well in which a wheel is pulled by horses or bulls, and it brings up the water. Once a horseman, riding through a forest, got tired and thirsty. He wanted his horse to drink water so he went to the well. The machine that draws water from the well was making a lot of noise, and that noise was very annoying. When the horseman took his horse there, the horse tried to run away from there.

The horseman said, "Please stop this sound, for my horse is running away."

The other man said, "If the sound stops, the water will also stop."

The horseman asked, "What to do?"

The other man replied, "Create a condition for your horse, so that the horse will drink water in this situation."

You have to create such a condition in this world to live happily. That requires human effort. Otherwise, the water will stop. You are all wanting to stop the sound, the noise, the pollution. Yet, if you go to the forest where there is nothing, you will be disturbed by the rush and roar of the wind.

You cannot find peace anywhere because there is no peace within. Peace does not mean that nobody should make noise. The noise will continue. Still you should have peace within. In all situations you should be peaceful, no matter what happens.

There is a problem with your concept of enjoyment. You need an object to enjoy, and then you depend on that object. You search for an object, and you work hard to obtain that object; then you are disappointed, because no object has the capacity to give you enjoyment. Enjoyment is a concept, an internal state, that you have to create. Enjoyment means every moment of life should be enjoyed.

You suffer from your thinking. Mind is like a small foot rule, that has no power to measure or fathom the deeper levels of your being. Mind and heart together, in a systematic way, can help you to attain contentment.

Contentment is the first and foremost virtue that should be cultivated. It comes only when you have done your duties to your fullest capacity without worrying for the results.

It is a virtue that always helps and never disappoints the seeker.

Do not keep undecided thoughts in your mind, for they disturb the equilibrium and create sickness. Life is very short and you should learn to enjoy every moment by remembering the Lord of Life, and always assuming your body to be a shrine of his living presence.

The Lord of Life is love. Never get sad. Be happy and take care of your happiness. Jump in joy without worrying for the future. Why remain serious? Let you learn to jump in joy and smile all the time. God bless you.

Happiness is within and the source is the center of consciousness, love, and wisdom.

Surrender

True enjoyment can never be had through the satisfaction of greed, but only through the surrender of the individual self to the universal Self.

When Christ was crucified, he never said, "Sorry, forgive me; release me from the cross." Christ had conviction. He had faith in God. He had so much faith in God that he didn't care what was happening to his body. This is something great. One can see the same thing in Buddha and Krishna. Buddha was very calm, and Krishna played the flute. Why the flute, when there are so many good instruments? Why did he not play another instrument, like the vina or the guitar?

A flute has many holes, just as all human beings have many weaknesses. However, a flute has nothing inside; it's empty. Christ said, "Empty thyself and I will fill thee."

Having many holes, if you become an instrument of God, a beautiful melody will come through. In all conditions, trust in God who is within you, witnessing your thoughts, speech, and actions.

Selflessness

Sit down and quietly think about what you have done in your life, because in the end, during the period of transition, you will have to face yourself. What have you done that is satisfying? Have you done anything selfless—totally selfless?

You go on doing your work and reaping the fruit, and then you hoard. In this way there can be no liberation. All the misery and chaos in the world is because of this. Somebody has an abundance; someone else doesn't have even a square meal. This disparity and the suffering that we find are created by ourselves.

How can you be peaceful if your neighbor's house is burning? How can you say you are at peace, and you don't feel any warmth? Those who understand life, understand the ripples of life. We are like ripples in the vast ocean of bliss.

If you are suffering, I am suffering, though I am not aware of it. How can I live without suffering? If my foot is suffering, definitely my whole being is suffering. We are all limbs of one huge, one great *prajapati* (being)—the whole universe. How can we live happily? Let us learn not to hoard, but just to give. To whom? Not to strangers. I'm not telling you something impractical. Give to those with whom you live.

Do not work for yourself; that is not the way of life. You will become selfish. Learn to work for others. If the wife learns to work for her husband, and the husband learns to work for his wife, they both will be happy. Problems come when they both become selfish, demanding, and expecting. Learn the path of selflessness. That is the only way of liberation.

Learn to give to each other, and then slowly that learning will expand to the whole universe. One day you will feel that the whole universe is your family, and you are one of the members of that family.

On the path of selflessness there is a great joy.

Selflessness is the singular expression of love.

Reality

The nature of Reality is a game of hide and seek, which is really the only game there is—now you see it and now you don't.

That which smiles through all faces is only One Reality and the same One is called One without second. There is only One that exists beneath all the forms of the world. There is only One—here, there, and everywhere—incomparable, changeless and everlasting.

It is said that as long as there exists the sense of duality, there also exists a space, and along with this comes a sense of time. These bind one under certain conditions and that is why there is fear, agony, and pain.

Had there been only One, what would there be to fear? Fear means acknowledging more than one at the same time. There exists only one Infinite loving itself, living with eternal joy all in One, all alone.

Walk alone and do not be lonely, for actually you are alone, which means all in One.

Time, Space, and Causation

It is important to know the three conditionings of the mind—time, space, and causation. You are afraid of someone because you acknowledge the existence of someone as different from you. If there is only One, who will be afraid of whom? When all desires are swallowed by only one wave, and when that wave alone exists, then there will be no time, space, or causation.

Time, space, and causation prevent you from realizing the unity in diversity.

The secrets of birth and death are revealed only to a fortunate few. It is a rare person who can lift the veil of time, space, and causation and then know that past, present, and future are but commas and semicolons in a long sentence without a period.

Karma

A person performs actions and is remunerated. The fruits of the actions motivate him to perform actions again, and then again he is rewarded. It becomes a cycle: the fruit arises out of the action, and the action out of the fruit. From time immemorial, life has proceeded in this manner. This is called the wheel of karma.

The law of karma is equally applicable to all. Our past samskaras are deeply rooted in the unconscious. These latent samskaras, or impressions, create various bubbles of thoughts that express themselves through our speech and actions.

It is possible for the aspirant to get freedom from these samskaras. Those who can burn these samskaras in the fire of nonattachment or knowledge, are free from the bondage created by them. It is like a burnt rope that has lost its binding power, though it still looks like a rope.

When latent impressions, though still in the unconscious, are burned by the fire of knowledge, they lose the power of germination, and will never grow. They are like roasted coffee beans. You can use them to brew a cup of coffee, but they have no power to grow.

No one can live without performing actions. When you perform actions, therein you reap the fruits of your actions. "As you sow, so shall you reap." Nobody can escape from this law.

When you reap the fruits of actions, those actions inspire you to perform more actions. Seemingly, there is no end. This creates a sense of helplessness. You cannot live without doing your duty, but when you do your duty, you find yourself caught in a whirlpool. You are not happy because duty makes you a slave.

The first thing you should learn is how to perform your actions, yet remain unaffected. Your duty should not give you stress and strain. It should not make you a slave.

You just need to change your attitude. Decide in the morning that you will do your duty lovingly, no matter what is expected.

If you think like that, you will find that you will not be tired at the end of the day as you usually are.

You have no alternative but to learn to love your duty. Then it becomes easy. If you do not love something, and yet you do it, it creates a division in your mind, and gives you stress. Learn to create love toward your duties. It can be done.

This is called human skill, human effort. Grace dawns when you have completed your human efforts. Therefore, do your human efforts with love. Learn to love.

It is possible to live perfectly on earth if one is able to work and to love—to work for what one loves, and to love what one is working at.

Nonattachment

If you really want to enjoy life and be happy, learn to practice and understand the philosophy of nonattachment.

Often Westerners think that the philosophy of non-attachment is impossible to practice. If you dive deep into the thinking process, you will find out that it is the only philosophy that helps.

Nonattachment is like a fire that can burn the binding power of past samskaras.

Nonattachment does not mean indifference or nonloving. Nonattachment and love are one and the same. Nonattachment gives freedom, but attachment brings bondage.

We have come from the unknown, we will return to the unknown. We should be grateful to the Lord, to Providence, for whatever we have. All the things of the world are meant for us and we have the right to use them. However, they are not ours, so we should not possess them. We have no right to establish ownership over the things we have, because they have been given to us to use, but they are not ours. We should use them as means, but we should not possess anything.

Learn to love all the things of the world, just as means but don't get attached to them. This is the secret—the philosophy of nonattachment.

Realization of the greatness of the Divine Force and the evanescence of the objects of the world results in pure *vairagya*, (dispassion). In the light of dispassion, or nonattachment, the aspirant attains freedom from his desires, whims, ambitions, and anxieties.

Being free from all distractions, he can undertake his practice wholeheartedly. Nonattachment enriches the nature of his practice. Practice combined with nonattachment helps him to continue his search until he reaches the goal.

Body

For any practice, an aspirant needs a strong, healthy body. The body is a great instrument and it should be taken care of properly.

Body is a projection of the mind. Any unrest in the body and nervous system is because of the mind. All of the body is in the mind, but the whole mind is not in the body. Anything that is in the body, the mind can know, but everything that is in the mind, body cannot know.

Physical health is considered to be an essential part of spiritual practice. An unhealthy body dissipates the mind, for all energy is directed to the body alone. A person with an unhealthy body does not have the energy to work on other aspects of his being.

Do not ignore your health. Body is an instrument and needs care. You are only a custodian of your body, breath, and mind. You are a pure soul—that is your real nature.

Four Fountains

If you analyze your mental attitudes, you will learn that those attitudes have roots deeper than mere thought. All the roots of your attitudes lie in the primitive fountains: food, sex, sleep, and self-preservation. If you really want to do sadhana and understand life and all the motivations that drive your life force, you must understand these four primitive fountains. Any problem that you have can be seen as related to these four sources.

FOOD

Dietary habits play an important role during sadhana. The sadhaka should be careful in having such a diet that does not pollute the body or agitate the nervous system. Sugar, salt, and fat should be curtailed. This will give you a joy that is derived from having a healthy body, breath, and mind.

Meditation should not be done when you are hungry, when you have overeaten, when you are tired or sleepy, or when you have any digestive problem. Select a suitable time and do it.

SEX

Many people live for sex, but when the opportunity comes, they cannot enjoy it. To experience this enjoyment, a person needs inner strength, and sometimes this is not there. Because of your food habits, or because you have not had enough rest, or do not know how to receive quality sleep, the body is not coordinated with the mind. Then you do not find yourself capable of doing those actions or behaving correctly with the other person when you are performing the sexual act, and you are always afraid.

Sex is very injurious if it is done without love. Some people do it like a mere physical exercise, but this is not a healthy way to approach sex. Your appetite for food is directly related to your body, but sex is not directly related to your body. Unless the thought or feeling comes into your mind, you cannot do sex. Sexuality occurs in the mind first, and then is expressed through the body. The desire for food occurs in the body first, and later food affects the mind.

SLEEP

The joy and pleasure that are provided by sleep are higher than any other pleasure, even food or sex.

The process of sleep provides rest for your body. Sleep is the state in which there is no content in the mind. If you make your mind free from conscious thinking, then you will go to sleep.

When you sleep, you often feel tired in the morning because you don't know how to have good quality sleep. Sometimes you cannot sleep because you have many anxieties and many issues to resolve. Even if you get the best sleep, you are still tired, because a part of yourself—your mind—still remains awake even when you go into a deep sleep.

Six or seven hours of sleep are good. To force oneself not to sleep is unhealthy.

Learn to wake up before sunrise, no matter what happens. Sloth or inertia is the greatest of all sins that hampers human progress.

Yogis practice a different sort of sleep called *yoga nidra*. Using yoga nidra, they voluntarily go to sleep. The sages understood that sleep does not give complete rest, and they discovered the method called yoga nidra in which you learn how to go to sleep and yet remain conscious.

In this state, even though you are in a deep sleep, you can record all the things occurring around you. The whole world believes that you are in a state of deep sleep, but actually you are fully aware and rested. In this method you can give your body complete rest, you can make your breath calm, and your mind serene.

SELF-PRESERVATION

Among all these forces, self-preservation is the strongest in both human beings and animals. If your life is threatened, you try to run away or seek to protect yourself with all your might and skill. There is an inherent fear in you that you might lose your body.

Fear exists because you fear losing what you have, or not gaining what you want.

When you learn something about these primitive fountains and how to cultivate them, then it becomes easier for you to control your diet, or your sleep, or sexuality. You should learn such self-control because you are a human being. To preserve and maintain your body, eat good food. Learn to sleep when you are tired.

Emotions

All of your emotions are related to the four primitive fountains. From these four urges or motivations rise the six main streams of emotions. *Kama* is the prime desire. The second stream is *krodha* or anger; if a desire is not fulfilled, you become angry and frustrated. If that same desire is fulfilled, you become puffed up with pride, *mada*, the third stream. If the desire is fulfilled, you become attached to the object that fulfilled your desire. That is *moha*. The next stream is *lobha*, which means that you become greedy and want more and more. When greed takes over, you do everything to feed *ahamkara* (ego); that prevents you from knowing your true Self.

Learn to have an even temperament by not losing your temper every now and then.

Sadness and loneliness are two companions on the path of sadhana. Your mantra is your great companion and you should never have to face moments of despair.

Emotions, if properly directed, can lead you to the highest state of ecstasy.

Mind

All sadhanas have a central theme: to have an orderly mind that does not create obstacles to the path of unfoldment within and does not hinder success in the external world.

The body is your physical instrument for living in the external world. Your mind or internal instrument is *antah-karana*. The antahkarana has four faculties that function in the interior world: *manas* (active mind), *chitta* (subconscious; storehouse or reservoir of subtle impressions or samskaras), *buddhi* (intellect), and ahamkara (ego, the sense of "I-am-ness" or individuality). Manas has five subtle senses and five gross senses to experience the external world—the world of objects. Coordinating the four faculties requires real effort and makes the mind creative, useful, and productive.

These four faculties of the mind should carefully be observed and their functioning should be analyzed in day to day life. As you keep accounts and know how much money you have spent and what your reserves are, you should also be able to keep account of the functions of the mind, both within and without.

Thought, action, and speech are the three main objects to be observed. How am I thinking and feeling, how am I speaking, and what motivates me to speak? Is the way that I am speaking helpful for me and others?

Thoughts come and go — do not brood on them. All thoughts have some origin. Find out from where they arise. If you throw a pebble into a lake, it will create ripples twice; first, when you throw it, and then again when it settles at the bottom of the lake.

Don't allow thoughts to settle in the lake of your mind. If an unpleasant thought comes, let it go. Don't get disturbed. Otherwise, you will lose the constant battle waged by your thoughts. Be friendly to your mind and don't create animosity toward it.

Any creative thought enveloped with selfless love and selfless service toward others, if not expressed and executed, is like a treachery and an abortion. If creative thoughts are not brought into action, frustration arises, which can create repression. One day that repression is projected through the body as a disease or 'dis-ease.'

Wherever you go, you will carry your mind with you. You have to start working with it, wherever you are. It is of no use knowing God, for he always exists everywhere. It is of no use knowing the world, because it is already there, and it has been known and analyzed by many in the past. The mystery lies between the two, and that is the mind. The mind can transport you to a higher realm of wisdom, and can come in touch with the collective consciousness.

Sadhana is for the mind. If the mind is trained, you have attained. If the mind is not purified with a definite discipline, it will suffer from the age-old epidemic of hallucination. Those who do not know sadhana, go on quarreling with the mind until the last breath of their lives.

Unless the mind is trained in a coordinated way by understanding all of its modifications, it remains unruly, disorderly, and enveloped in its primitive dharma. An untrained mind interferes with the spontaneous feelings arising from the heart.

Mind is the cause of both bondage and liberation. A one-pointed mind can help one go within and unveil the mystery of inner life, whereas an undisciplined mind remains dissipated.

An outwardly oriented mind runs from one object to another, hoping to find peace and happiness in the external world. Lacking inner awareness, the mind refuses the guidance and inspiration of the subtle Divine Force. A mind not guided by divine illumination stands as a wall between the aspirant and his goal. Having such a mind, one fails to study the inner dimensions of life, and as a result, considers the external world to be the sole reality.

To attain perfection here and now, one must undertake some spiritual discipline. Without practice one cannot attain control over the modifications of the mind. Unless the mind is made one-pointed, one cannot unfold one's inner potentials.

The method of making the mind one-pointed is called meditation. Through meditation, an aspirant withdraws his mind from the external world, focuses on a given internal object, and develops an interest in delving within.

Once an aspirant has attained freedom from the distractions originating in the conscious part of the mind, he can have a better grasp of the thought constructs that originate from the unconscious mind. Through undisturbed, prolonged practice, a student dives deep and becomes familiar with his inherent potentials. He observes how the experiences of the external world are a mere reflection of the inner world.

There is no conflict in life. Conflict lies in the mind. The mind needs training. Even though a trained mind is not capable of leading one to the summit, it will remove all the obstacles along the way. A free mind is the grace of the Lord.

When an aspirant has understood the conscious part of the mind, and has attained mastery over it, he naturally performs his actions skillfully and efficiently. Compared to the unconscious, the conscious part of mind is very small; however, there is close interaction between the unconscious and the conscious mind.

Enjoy life moment to moment and do not get disturbed. That which is not going to happen will not happen, and that which is going to happen is going to happen. Therefore, tranquility should not be disturbed. A mind that is balanced and tranquil cannot be a workshop of the devil.

Never identify yourself with your mind, its objects, emotions, speech, or actions. The doer is different from the deeds. Never identify with your actions, thoughts, and emotions, but remain in eternal delight by establishing yourself in your essential nature that is peace, happiness, and bliss.

Ego

A person walking on the path of self-transformation should be aware of the dangers of egoism. Even while practicing the great virtues of truthfulness and nonviolence, a person can feed the ego. The ego related to the realm of spirituality is more subtle and injurious than the ego related to one's worldly success.

During the period of seeking, the student may become too intellectual, ignoring *sahaja bhava* (spontaneous intuition); conversely, he may become too emotional; ignoring reason. An emotional trip is as dangerous as an intellectual trip; each feeds the ego.

A person becomes a slave to his ego when he thinks of selfish gains. A selfish person dwells in a state of doubt since his conscience constantly reminds him of his wrong attitude. On the one hand, he is pulled by his selfish desires, and on the other, he is alarmed by his inner voice. He is torn apart by these two forces.

Do not ever condemn yourself in any way. Learn to appreciate and admire yourself, but see that you do not feed your ego. It is the arch enemy on the path, though it can be polished with some effort.

Acknowledge your weak points, let the power of discrimination counsel your ego, and make a strong resolution to overcome your weaknesses. While working on the removal of weaknesses, you have to be very vigilant. Ego does not want its weaknesses exposed. The more you hide your weaknesses, the more they grow. Remind yourself that you are on the path of inner purification and self-discovery. It requires great courage. Stand firm during this internal battle, and support your Atman, even at the cost of dismounting the ego and all its retinue.

A human being is miserable if he fails to unfold and use his inner potentials. In order to unfold his inner potentials, he must purify the ego or surrender it to the higher Reality. After renouncing slavery to the ego, he can emerge from the confines of body, senses, and mind.

Only a profound method of meditation can help to purify the ego. A purified ego does not create barriers.

By practicing diligently, one may attain concentration of mind, one may speak the truth, and one may serve others, but one cannot realize the Truth unless one surrenders one's ego to the higher Self. Only after rising above egocentric awareness, can one find the universe within. Only then can one learn to love all and exclude none. One who does not love one's fellow beings, cannot love God at all.

Humanity is suffering from ego-born differences and inequality. People discriminate against their own brothers and sisters simply on the basis of race, religion, caste, or complexion. In order to be free from these problems, a political settlement alone is not enough.

When all human beings understand that their suffering has been brought on by ego, only then will they resolve all their differences. They will throw aside the confinements of race, caste, religion, and sectarian feelings. Instead of identifying themselves with a particular group or community, they will identify themselves with all human beings. They will love all as their own family members.

The ego is very useful in helping you to function in the world, but it's not very useful as far as deeper happiness is concerned. The ego is that which separates you from the Reality, from the Truth, from the ultimate Source.

The most important step toward self-transformation is to shed one's ego, to surrender it to the higher Reality, and thereby attain the light of discrimination and pure faith.

Once ego surrenders itself to the highest Truth, you have attained victory, and spiritual illumination is yours. Soon after the victory over ego, all other virtues, such as humility, love, selflessness, compassion, and kindness, spontaneously unfold. These virtues are prerequisites for self-transformation. When these virtues blossom, a human being becomes a saint. These saintly qualities send a silent invitation to the Lord of Life.

Discrimination

Manas is not an appropriate tool for searching for the Truth. The heart also is not competent. The buddhi (intellect), the faculty of discrimination, is qualified to guide you. When the buddhi, the finest aspect of the antahkarana (internal instrument), is sharpened, and a coordination is established between the buddhi and the different aspects of the mind, then one can have a perfect and orderly mind. Such a mind, when coordinated with the power of the emotions, is able to penetrate into the deeper levels of your being.

As a human being you have inherited a vast treasure of knowledge. You can have access to that treasure only if the mind is made one-pointed and inward. Beyond manas is the intellect. The power of intellect guides the functions of the mind.

Unlike manas that always remains in a state of doubt, the intellect is endowed with the power of discrimination and decision. The mind, fully guided by the higher faculty of intellect, becomes a great instrument to achieve peace and happiness. However, you should remember that a dissipated mind never listens to the intellect. The intellect can guide only a one-pointed mind. Therefore, the most important step in spiritual practice is to make the mind one-pointed, so that it can be guided by the decisive faculty called intellect.

The power of discrimination is the greatest of all benevolent forces within. With the help of contemplation and meditation, one should unfold this power and learn to distinguish right actions from unwholesome ones.

One should execute the power of discrimination to analyze one's inner states. The recognition of strengths and weaknesses should not be allowed to feed the ego, or lead one toward self-condemnation. The purpose of inner analysis is to unfold the good qualities and remove the weaknesses.

One who lacks the power of discrimination performs his actions without being aware of their consequences. Most of the time, he is driven by his desires, whims, and primitive urges. He usually does not know what truth is, and even if he knows, he fails to practice it in his thoughts, speech, and actions.

Without perfect faith in the higher Reality, he cannot attain freedom from his own anxiety and insecurity. Without discrimination and faith, he may perform his actions, but he lives in a state of doubt.

Unless these two principles—discrimination and faith—are fully unfolded, one cannot rise above the spheres of manas and ego. He cannot distinguish right actions spontaneously, and cannot perform his actions wholeheartedly.

He who listens to the voice of the inner soul and performs actions under the guidance of discrimination, rises above egocentric awareness. He attains foresight and the power of discrimination guides him on the path of righteousness.

Through uninterrupted practice of meditation and contemplation, he one day attains illumination. His whole life is driven by the power of discrimination and faith, and he enters into the kingdom of the eternal heart.

Consciousness

The word consciousness is often used in modern psychology and philosophical literature. It is used for *Atmajnana*, the direct knowledge that we receive from our Atman. *Jiva Atma* is the individual soul, and *Param Atma* is pure consciousness.

From the center of consciousness flows the life force in various degrees and grades. With the following simile, you will clearly understand. When a lamp has many shades, the light is very dim. When you take off the shades, one by one, finally you find the center of light.

Similarly, the soul is the center of consciousness and the knowledge that flows through manas, chitta, buddhi and ahamkara, and then through the senses, is called consciousness. This is the light of knowledge that flows from its source, the fountainhead of light and life, the Atman.

I have a firm faith that here, in life on earth where opposites clash together, the general level of consciousness can be raised. The development of intelligence and physical power and moral ethics are equally necessary for a human being to grow and unfold himself for the purpose of living.

That which obstructs the human being is the mind and the wall created by individual habits and superficial conventions; otherwise the human being is complete.

What is unique in the human being is the development of consciousness that gradually expands and deepens the realization of his immortal being, the limitless eternal and perfect.

Prayer

Many students who meditate think that prayer is not needed, because they don't understand what prayer is. Why do you want to pray?

From morning until evening you pray, "Lord, give me this, Lord, give me that." What are you actually doing? You are feeding your ego, which is a bad habit. This is called egocentric prayer. Human beings, tossed by desires and wants, have become victims of egocentric prayer, which really makes them beggars. It is still prayer, and so it is better than not doing anything at all.

Pray in your own language to the Lord of Life, who is seated in the inner chamber of your being. He knows you better than anyone else. He guides you, protects you, and helps you.

Pray to the Lord of Life in your heart to give you strength and wisdom, so that you can understand life from all perspectives.

It is essential twice a day, morning and evening, to pray. Prayer is a petition for extra energy for our success. To whom to pray? God is the source of all energies, the center, the powerhouse of light, life, and love. Through prayer we can reach to that powerhouse and draw the energy for expanding the field of our mind and the horizon of our consciousness.

You are praying to someone who is not body, breath, and mind, but who is seated beyond and behind this mortal frame, whose nucleus is within you and whose expansion is the universe. There is only one absolute Reality that exists, and the same exists within you.

You want to reach and touch some higher force whom you call God. You make your mind one-pointed with a desire that motivates you to pray; absorbed in your desire for prayer, the mind becomes calm. When the mind is calm, the Great Majesty reveals itself to the mind, and the purpose of prayer is accomplished.

There are many steps of prayer, and the first is to say a few mantras and then to mentally remember those mantras; then wait for the answer to be received. Every prayer is answered.

When you learn to meditate, making the body steady and still, the breath serene, and the mind free from turmoil, this will lead you to a state of inner experience. You come in touch with something higher and receive the knowledge that is not from the mind, but from beyond—from deep within.

You should learn to meditate with the feeling that the body is a shrine and the inner dweller, the Lord of Life, is God. Mind is a sadhaka and learns to surrender its manners, moods, and weapons by saying, "I have no capacity. My abilities are limited. Help me Lord, give me power, so that I can solve all the problems boldly and without getting flattened like a ball of clay, or crumbled as a house of cards is crumbled by the touch of a finger."

In this way the mind forms a habit of depending on the Lord of Life, instead of leaning on the 'mere I.' The 'mere I' is the ego, and the 'real I' is God within. This inward process is meditation cum prayer. All other prayers are futile, enveloped by wants and desires, fully colored by selfishness, and are just for the sake of pleasing the ego.

Never pray for anything selfish. Pray to the Lord so that your mind receives energy and the Lord motivates you to do what is right for you and for others. That which cannot be accomplished through any other means can be accomplished through prayer. There is a beautiful verse in the Bible, "Knock and it shall be opened unto you." It is not written how many times one has to knock!

Prayer and repentance are the greatest purifiers that purify the way of life and lead us to Self-realization. Prayer without repentance does not help much.

Prayers are always answered, therefore, pray with all your mind and heart.

The Spiritual Heart

The human being is said to have three hearts. One is physical and can be dissected by the surgeon's knife. The psychic heart is that heart that is led by an orderly mind. The spiritual heart has control over heart and mind both. It is not subject to sorrow, pain and misery.

In the human body there are two hemispheres—the upper and the lower—and there are seven spheres. That which connects both hemispheres is called *anahata chakra*. This is the spiritual heart. It is located at the space between the two breasts.

This chakra is represented by two interlocking triangles. The triangle that is pointing upward represents human endeavor, and the triangle pointing downward is the grace of God, or the descending force. That which is pointed upward is the ascending force. Together they form a star. The Jewish tradition calls it the star of David, the Christian tradition calls it the cross of the Sacred Heart, and the Hindu tradition calls it the anahata chakra. When the mind is focused on the spiritual heart, it attains a state of deep concentration.

Meditation

Meditation is a process of purifying the mind and making it one-pointed, inward, and tranquil. Through the method of meditation, the mind will help you to fathom the deeper levels of your being and lead you to the highest state of realization.

As an aspirant, it is always wise to be vigilant and firm in practicing meditation. Do not expect too much right in the beginning. There is no instant method of meditation. Modern students expect immediate results from meditation and this expectation causes them to fantasize, imagine, and hallucinate many things that they think are spiritual experiences. These experiences are actually products of their subconscious minds. As a result, they become frustrated and imbalanced, and either they stop meditating, or they start following strange methods that are harmful to their progress.

Meditation is a technique that has only one way, and that is a scientific way that is very precise and clear. If you learn how to systematically practice meditation, it will not take much time for you to reach the summit, provided you know the whole technique.

First thing is to have a strong desire, a burning desire within. When you have a burning desire to do your meditation, that burning desire leads you. Sankalpa shakti is needed. "Today I will sit in meditation. No one has the power to disturb me! Thought is a product of the mind. I do not belong to thought."

If you learn to go beyond the jabbering of your mind, and can go to the deeper aspects of your consciousness, then body, breath, and mind will not come in your way.

They come in your way because you have not trained them, because you have not decided to do meditation. Once and for all you should learn to decide, and fix up a time for meditation in the morning and before you go to bed.

You have been taught to see and examine things in the external world. Nobody has taught you to see and find within. There is no other way but the way of meditation. No object of the world has the power to give you what meditation can give you.

Don't meditate if you are not inclined to meditate. If you want to meditate, you have to form a habit, because habit weaves your character and personality. If you really want to know who you are, you have to take off all the masks, one after the other. You have to be totally naked. You have to be in the fire. If you are prepared to do that, you can learn to tread the path of meditation.

In the external world there is no object that can make you happy, because all objects are subject to change, death, decay, and decomposition. That which is subject to change, and is not everlasting, can never give you happiness. It can give you only momentary joy.

That momentary joy is evidence enough that there is something that is called joy. You are searching in the wrong place. If you receive everlasting joy, and if you have attained everlasting joy, then you'll be free. It is for that freedom and for that great joy that you live.

When you sit in meditation, I advise you not to worry about seeing lights. You have to learn to make your abode in complete darkness, so that you can see that gentle light. Do not worry if you don't see any light or have any visions or experiences.

If you have patience and learn to sit still, the center of life and light will start revealing itself to you. Until then, imagining superficial lights is harmful. Learn to be in the darkness waiting for the light to be revealed.

Having no experience in meditation is the right experience. If you systematically follow the meditation method, there is no chance for you to worry and feel that you are not progressing.

Whenever you are meditating, or making effort to meditate, you are doing something. Don't say and don't think that you are not reaping the fruits of your actions. It is not possible. It is unscientific that you do something and you don't get anything. Every action has its reaction.

If you systematically learn to meditate, you will find that the faculty of discrimination, the buddhi, will help you in all walks of life, both within and without.

You have to pay attention to four important points: building determination, learning to pray, learning to meditate according to instructions, and not allowing your mind to be stained by self-created guilt that destroys the inner spiritual potentials.

Learn to be spiritual in your daily life by doing selfless action. Learn to meditate every day, a few minutes. Don't become a hypocrite, sitting for a long time and hallucinating. Meditate for a few minutes, and enjoy life. Learn to meditate and learn to be here and now. Meditational therapy is the highest.

Meditation is self-effort, a probe into inner life, and will reveal all the secrets to you in time to come.

Stillness

Meditation is a journey without movement. In the external world you have to move in order to go ahead, in meditation you don't move, yet you attain. First thing you should learn is how to be still physically. Take one month for stilling the body. You will find that you are able to easily arrest the twitching, tremors, and jerks, of your body.

When the body is still, you will find great joy and confidence. Learn to enjoy that stillness. No matter what joys you have experienced so far, the highest of all joys is stillness.

Learn to sit in a quiet and calm place every day at the same time with determination. Learn not to move, yet remain comfortable. Ask your mind to make the body still. There should not be any strain or rigidity in it.

If you know how to sit still for some time, then you will be able to make your breath serene. Without serene breath and a tranquil mind, there is no spirituality. Why do we make the body still, the breath serene, and the mind calm? We do it so they will not disturb us.

Make a *mudra* with your fingers by gently touching the thumb to the index finger, then place the hands over the knees. This mudra, or gesture, creates a circuit in the body that prevents the outward dissipation of your energy.

Keep your head, neck, and trunk straight, and then gently close your eyes and mentally observe the stillness of your body. Your body may begin tilting forward. Your inner feelings and frustrations cause your body to move.

The first few days you should learn to watch the stillness. Enjoy the stillness. Great joy will spring out of stillness.

Therefore, the first step is to be still. I assure you, you will enjoy it.

Power is in stillness as much as in movement.

Posture

You will have to choose a posture for yourself. The posture that you use for meditation should be one in which you are comfortable and steady, and one that allows you to keep the head, neck, and trunk aligned.

There are a few traditional meditation postures. *Sukhasana* (easy posture) is the simplest cross-legged posture for sitting on the floor. If your legs are flexible, you may find *swastikasana* (auspicious pose) more comfortable. It is not advised to use *padmasana* (lotus pose), because it is not possible to apply *mula bandha* (root lock) in this posture.

The finest of all postures for meditation is called *siddhasana* (accomplished pose). In this pose, if you gently and gradually practice it, you will find that your body becomes like a statue. The accomplished pose should not be used by beginners.

Whichever posture you are using for meditation, from the very beginning you should learn to apply mula bandha. You have to contract the anal sphincters and hold the contraction, until your posture is applied.

Breath

At least three times a day, you should practice some simple breathing exercises. Regulation of the breath helps one to easily attain control of the modifications of the mind.

No breathing exercise can be mastered without deep diaphragmatic breathing. Gently push in your abdomen to your fullest capacity, sealing your lips and exhaling from the nostrils; then relax your abdomen without any force and inhale.

When you push in your abdomen comfortably, that pushes in the greatest of all muscles, called the diaphragm. The diaphragm in turn pushes against the lungs and helps the lungs to expel carbon dioxide, or used up gas. As you gently relax the abdomen to inhale, the diaphragm also relaxes and the lungs can expand fully.

Exhale and inhale according to your fullest capacity at least ten times. It will help you to calm down passive and negative moods.

Practice five to ten minutes, three times a day, in *shavasana* (corpse pose). While practicing diaphragmatic breathing in shavasana, contract your anus gently, so that the rectal and vaginal muscles do not remain loose. This exercise is *aswini mudra*. It is very useful because that area does not get exercise. This will prevent the *apana vayu* flow from being disturbed.

When you are doing breathing exercises, pay full attention. Attention is the key to both breathing and meditation.

When you meditate place your hands on your knees and make the finger lock by uniting the thumb and first finger. Survey your body from head to toe, and see that every part of your body is fully relaxed.

Gently close your eyes, and then again observe mentally. Let the mind learn to have awareness of the body.

From a lack of practice, the legs may become numb. Gradually, this will vanish.

By practicing yogic breathing exercises, one attains balance between inhalation and exhalation. Regulation of inhalation and exhalation helps one to still the body and mind.

Breath Awareness

When the posture is steady, the body is still and comfortable, and you are breathing diaphragmatically, the next step is breath awareness—observing the flow of your breath.

Let your mind be focused on the breath and allow the mind to flow with the breath. The breath should not be jerky or shallow, it should not be noisy, and you should not uselessly expand the natural pause between inhalation and exhalation.

Breath is a barometer to measure one's inner state. When you observe that your breath is serene, deep, and without any unnecessary pause, you will experience a sense of great comfort and joy.

The more the mind is made steady and one-pointed, the more one experiences peace and happiness. There are several ways of making the mind steady and one-pointed. Among them, concentration on inhalation and exhalation is considered to be the best.

Concentration on the flow of breath is one of the best ways to attain control over the modifications of the mind. When all the modifications cease, and the mind is calm and tranquil, one finds great joy within. When the mind is free from all distractions, and starts travelling inward, an aspirant begins to unveil the mystery of multilevel reality. Through a one-pointed mind, one gains knowledge of the inner world. This knowledge is superior to that derived from perception, inference, or testimony.

You will find extraordinary joy when you have coordinated the mind with the breath. Gradually you move your mind from the breath to sound awareness. The sound *so-hum* is the best to concentrate upon. When you remember so-hum, *so* is the sound of inhalation and *hum* is the sound of exhalation.

With your eyes closed, focus your mind on the lowest center along the spinal column, called *muladhara*. Inhale as though you are inhaling from the root of the spinal column, while inhaling the sound so; then exhale with the sound hum, as though you are exhaling from the crown of your head to your toes.

In this way the ratio of exhalation to inhalation will be double—inhale four and exhale eight. Do it ten times after practicing diaphragmatic breathing. After a few days, you will find your breath has become very calm.

Whenever you are in great joy, you will find that the mind is calm and the breath is serene. You can never remain in joy and you can never be happy, unless there is perfect coordination between the breath and mind.

Life is breath and breath is life.

Mantra

You often close your eyes and sit down and you don't know what to do next; then you start remembering your mantra. You can remember your mantra all the time, but that's not very systematic. It will take a long time for you. You're doing *japa*, but you're doing it halfheartedly. If you do the same thing with full concentration, it will definitely give you results.

When you remember your mantra, you should remember it with all your feeling. You should know about your mantra—understand what your mantra is.

Remember your mantra as silently as possible, and it will help you tremendously. Let your mind be led by your mantra and let it become a part of your life.

Remember your mantra—slowly, gently—and follow it. The sound will take you to the soundless state that is beyond body, breath, and mind. That is what meditation is.

The Witness

In my childhood my master used to tell me again and again to meditate. I wanted to, but for lack of practice I couldn't. I always complained, exactly like you, that the mind runs here and there.

He said, "It's the dharma of the mind to run here and there. Why are you worried about somebody's dharma?"

Dharma means duty or nature. It is the inherent nature of mind to flow. Those who think the mind should be stopped, do not understand anything about the mind. Only a part of the mind can be brought under your control, and that is called conscious mind. The conscious mind is that part of the mind that functions in your daily life during the waking state.

In the initial stages of meditation, a student learns to calm the conscious mind. When the conscious part of the mind is relaxed, a train of thoughts comes, disturbing inner tranquility. At that moment, the student should remain firm and should not identify with those past impressions. He should pay full attention to the object of concentration; that will help him remain uninvolved with the memories of the past. Gradually, he crosses that phase and starts experiencing the unalloyed Truth. The experience of the Truth is pure in itself.

The conscious mind receives impressions from the world through the senses, and also from the unconscious part of the mind. If you stop the input of external sensations, the thought patterns that are stored in the unconscious start coming forward. There is only one way to deal with these thought patterns—to let go. You have to decide that no matter what happens, no thought will be allowed to be entertained.

You will find that the thoughts in which you are interested will stay for a long time, and the thoughts that you do not find interesting, will quickly disappear. By observing your thoughts you can see where your interests lie, where your thoughts are running, and what the grooves of your thoughts are. You can inspect your thinking process. Slowly you will become an inspector instead of getting involved as a victim.

Why do you find difficulty in meditation? You want to control your mind, but it doesn't cooperate. It always goes against you and tricks you. When you talk about sadhana, you are talking about how to deal with the mind and its two assistants—speech and action.

What you need to learn is not to control the mind, but how to observe the mind. You have to strengthen that particular faculty that has the capacity to observe everything.

First you should learn to witness things, even in the external world. You've formed a habit of getting involved with everything. If somebody says you are beautiful, you smile and feel happy. If somebody says you are bad, you feel sad. You get involved in anyone's suggestion, whether it is right or wrong. Your life is led by other people's opinions. This means you cannot form your own opinion, or you have not known the technique of forming your own opinion, and expressing your own opinion.

When you meditate you should decide that no matter what happens, any thought that comes will not be able to disturb you. When the mind brings forward material from the unconscious, or from the external world, do not get involved in it, just observe.

It's not a friend or foe who disturbs you. It is the thought of your friend or foe that disturbs you. Learn to observe; learn to witness your thinking process.

For a few minutes every day you should learn to be still; then observe your breath; and then observe your mind. Observe the train of thoughts, coming from the unknown, and going toward the unknown. Just observe. Decide that no matter what happens, no thoughts will be able to distract you.

Observing means you are different from the seen. You become a seer; you don't get involved. When you get involved you are a normal human being; when you don't get involved, you are a seer. If you learn not to be affected by your mind in meditation, you will never be affected by your thoughts, and nobody can influence you in the external world.

Weakness means a weak mind; strength means a strong mind. A strong mind does not mean you should not listen to others. That's called obstinate mind. Mental strength means your mind is not tossed by anything adversely.

In the Mundaka Upanishad there is a parable:

Two identical birds that are eternal companions perch in the very same tree. One eats many fruits of various tastes. The other only witnesses without eating.

The two birds are the individual self and pure Atman. The individual self identifies itself with the objects of the world and enjoys the fruits of actions and the experiences of the pairs of opposites, such as pain and pleasure. Pure Atman only witnesses and remains absolutely unaffected by the taint of enjoyment and suffering.

Knowledge

There are two ways of gaining knowledge: through direct experience, and from external sources. The knowledge gained from direct experience is complete, self-evident, and fulfilling. The knowledge gained from external sources is incomplete, fragmented, requires evidence for its validity, and is not satisfying. Direct knowledge alone should be considered valid. Direct experience is the highest of all ways of gaining knowledge. All other means are only fragmentary.

On the path of Self-realization, purity, one-pointedness, and control of the mind are essentials. An impure mind hallucinates and creates obstacles, but an orderly mind is an instrument for direct experience.

Generally we keep gathering knowledge from the external world in the form of information. The world around us is an ever present teacher. Our mother is our first teacher, then our father, and then our brothers and sisters. Later we learn from the children with whom we play, from teachers at school, and from the writers of books. No matter what we have learned, we have not learned a single thing independently. Still we call ourselves learned. Realized sages pity us because we have not learned anything independently. All our ideas are the ideas of others.

It is shocking to realize that whatever we have learned so far is not ours. That is why it is not satisfying. Even if we have mastered an entire library, still it doesn't satisfy us.

However, by experimenting with the knowledge that we have acquired from outside, we can move a step toward enlightenment.

By gaining worldly knowledge, we develop the skills that are useful for gathering means and resources. A resourceful person can then have a better chance to direct his energies inward to explore the subtler and more glorious dimensions of life. The knowledge gained in the form of information serves a noble purpose as long as it inspires us to gain direct experience.

No matter how impressive it may appear, if knowledge gained from the external world doesn't help us loosen the knots of worldly snares, it is in vain. In most cases, the more information we gain, the more burdened our life becomes. By gaining such knowledge we become educated, but not enlightened. The indirect knowledge that we gain from years of studies and vocational training is of course informative, and to some extent, useful, but not fulfilling.

All wise people throughout history have gone through great pains in order to know Truth directly. They were not satisfied by the mere opinions of others. They were not frightened away from this quest by the defenders of orthodoxy and dogma who persecuted, and sometimes even executed them, because their conclusions were different.

Direct experience is the final test of the validity of knowledge. When you have known the Truth directly, you have the best kind of confirmation. Most of you go to your friends and give your viewpoint. You are seeking confirmation in their opinions. Whatever you think, you want others to confirm it by agreeing with you, to say, "Yes, what you think is right." Someone else's opinion is no test of truth.

When you know Truth directly you do not need to ask your neighbors or your teacher. You don't have to seek confirmation in books.

Spiritual Truth does not need an external witness. As long as you doubt, it means you have yet to know. Tread the path of direct experience until you attain that state where everything is clear, until all of your doubts are resolved. Direct experience alone has access to the source of real knowledge.

We all know what to do and what not to do, but it is very difficult to learn how to be. Real knowledge is found not in knowing, but rather in being. Knowing is mere information. Practice leads to direct experience and valid knowledge.

The outside world can soothe and stimulate your mind and senses, but peace, wisdom, and knowledge come from within. That knowledge that we gain through books is valid in the mundane world, but the real knowledge is found within.

The best of knowledge comes through revelations, not through the mind. It is a flood of knowledge that overwhelms the whole being. When you can calm the mind, then that knowledge will come to you.

Enlightenment

Through self-analysis you come to know that you are not only a physical being, you are not only a breathing being, you are not only a sensing being, and you are not only a thinking being. You have a body, breath, senses, and mind, but you are something more than this.

People continue to build shrines, chapels, churches, and temples. You don't have to do this, just realize that you are a living shrine. The day you have attained the knowledge that the Lord lives within you, you will be in samadhi. All questions will be answered, all problems will be resolved.

As you progress in the practice of meditation, the mind becomes one-pointed and calm. Such a tranquil mind begins working in accordance with the intellect. No contradiction remains between the functions of mind and intellect. The impurities of mind, such as doubt and conflict that usually pollute the intellect, are removed from the mind. Intellect is no longer disturbed by the activities of the mind, and you experience an extraordinary inner peace.

Intellect is described in the scriptures as a mirror that is in very close proximity to Atman. As long as the mirror of intellect is clean, it reflects the clearest and least distorted vision of Atman. If the intellect is colored with the thoughts and feelings of the lower mind, it presents a distorted picture of the Atman. According to the

Upanishads, one should remove all the impurities from the mind, and make the mind free from all doubts and conflicts, so the intellect can be as pure as crystal.

An intellect free from the influences of the lower mind finds itself in a well balanced state. Only such an intellect is capable of making an aspirant self-confident and self-reliant. Through such an intellect, the meditator knows that the goal of life is not far away.

An intellect free from the disturbances of the lower mind attains the illumination of the Atman from above. Darkness belonging to the realms of mind and senses cannot exist in the light of an illumined intellect. In the absence of all thought constructs, the lower mind merges into the intellect.

When intellect is absorbed in the Divine Light, that is the state of samadhi, the state of fearlessness and immortality. As long as one takes refuge in worldly objects, the body, pranic energy, and the forces of the lower mind, one remains a victim of old age, death, and rebirth.

When the intellect is fully illuminated by the light of the Atman, one becomes fearless. At the dawn of spiritual enlightenment, the mind and the intellect find their place in the kingdom of Atman, and one thereby attains freedom from the pairs of opposites such as pain and pleasure. This is the highest state of freedom.

When an individual learns to expand his consciousness or unites with the universal consciousness, then he no longer remains within the bounds of his karma. He is totally free.

You should do your duty in the world with love, and that alone will contribute significantly to your progress in the path of enlightenment.

One who dwells in the domain of the Atman does not belong to a particular family, society, or nation. Rather, he is part of all of humanity. He loves the welfare of all, as much as he loves his own Atman.

Peace

Peace has perhaps never been experienced by the world. It is a narrow gulf, a gap between two wars. As long as two diverse principles exist in the universe, there can never be peace.

Peace is only an ambition, a desire, and a thought of those who do not understand the diverse ways of the two principles in life and the universe. Sages, having understood the Reality, have attained a state of nonattachment and wisdom and remain unaffected by the turbulence of life.

There is no other way for peace but to go to the deep silence where She resides in Her Majesty, full of peace.

The Ancient Traveler

The most ancient traveler in the universe is love. It is love that travels from the unknown to the known, from eternity to eternity.

Those who want to realize the greatest delight should realize themselves in others. This is the definition of true love.

The spirit of love is boundless and emancipates our being from illusory bonds and superimpositions. It is unity that will lead us to Truth. That which is the beginning and the end of the phenomenal world is divine.

Loving somebody does not mean hating others. Remember this. If you love somebody, that means loving all. Your love should travel toward expansion, not toward contraction.

Learn to love others and demonstrate your love through selfless action. This is very important. Try not to hurt others through speech. Dark words have no capacity to contain real feeling and love, for they are not containers. Love is immortal and needs an immortal container. People say that it is expressed through the heart; therefore, the heart is the center of love. I deny that. The soul, actually, is the real container of love, for the soul alone is the most ancient traveler, and so is love. They are one and the same.

There are two types of love: one can be expressed, and one can never be expressed or explained. Anything that can be explained is not deep love. Though we all try to express it in a million ways, it is in vain.

There is only one Reality without second, without any space, time, or causation. We call it love.

You talk of love. You always aspire to have love. You always want to be loved. If you really want to know what love is, there are two phrases: as life is to live, love is to give.

Usually love is mingled with selfishness. I need something, so I say, "I love you." You need something, so you say you love me. This is what we call love in the world. Real love is when you do actions selflessly and spontaneously, and you don't expect any reward.

Reverence is the first rung on the ladder of love.

Love is not mere contemplation of the truth, but suffering for it. Suffering is not punishment, but a reward and a gift of love. The reward is received when you are no more there.

May we light the fire of love that burns out the ego and enables us to pass from fearful fragmentation to fearless fullness in the changeless whole.

God bless you. God loves you, I love you, let you learn to love yourself.

Gurudeva

A time comes when the seeker goes through a period of argumentation with herself and cannot decide. At this time a real preceptor is needed. How will you find the right master? No one can search for a preceptor. There is a saying in the scriptures: "When the disciple is prepared, the master appears." This happens only because of samskaras. Teacher and student samskaras are very ancient and strong.

If you are not prepared, he will be there, but you won't notice or respond. If you do not know what a diamond is, the diamond may be there, but you ignore it and pass it by, taking it to be just a piece of glass. Further, if you do not know the difference, you may acquire a piece of glass, think that it is a diamond, and cherish it your whole life.

A genuine spiritual teacher, one who is assigned to teach according to tradition, searches out good students. He looks for certain signs and symptoms; he wants to know who is prepared. No student can fool a master. The master easily perceives how well the student is prepared. If he finds that the student is not yet ready, he will gradually prepare him for the higher teachings. When the wick and oil are properly prepared, the master lights the lamp. That is his role. The resulting light is divine.

You need someone who can guide and help you. You need an external guru as a means to attain the guru within you. Sometimes you may become egotistical and decide that you don't need a guru. That is just ego talking.

You will never meet a bad guru if you are a good student. The reverse is also true; if you are a bad student, you won't meet a good guru. Why should a good guru assume responsibility for a bad student? Nobody collects garbage. If you are in search of a guru, search within first. To become a yogi means to know your own condition here and now, to work with yourself. Don't grumble because you don't have a teacher. Ask whether you deserve one. Are you capable of attracting a teacher? Are you prepared to be guided?

There is a vast difference between an ordinary teacher and a spiritual master or guru. That which dispels the darkness of ignorance is called guru. In the West the word guru is often misused. In India this word is used with reverence and is always associated with holiness and the highest wisdom. It is a very sacred word. It is seldom used by itself, but always with its suffix, *deva*. Deva means "bright being." An enlightened master or guru is called *gurudeva*.

When a student goes to a guru, he takes a bundle of dry sticks. With reverence and love he bows and says, "Here, I offer this." That indicates that he is surrendering himself with all his mind, action, and speech with a single desire to attain the highest wisdom.

The guru burns those sticks and says, "Now I will guide you and protect you in the future." Then he initiates the student on various levels and gives him the disciplines to practice. The guru imparts a word and says, "This will be an eternal friend to you. Remember this word. It will help you." Then he explains how to use the mantra. That is called mantra initiation.

You may try your best to do something for him, but you cannot, because he doesn't need anything. You wonder, "Why is he doing so much for me? What does he want from me?"

He wants nothing, for what he is doing is his duty, the purpose of his life. If he guides you, he is not obliging you; he is doing his work. He cannot live without doing his duty. Genuine gurus cannot live without selflessness, for selfless love is the very basis of their enlightenment. They radiate life and light from the unknown corners of the world. The world does not know them, and they do not want recognition.

Such people are called gurus. They guide humanity. As the sun shines and lives far above, the guru gives spiritual love and remains unattached.

Guru is not a physical being. Those who think of the guru as a body or as a man do not understand this pious word. If a guru comes to think that his power is his own, then he is a guide no more. The guru is tradition, he is a stream of knowledge. That stream of knowledge goes through many channels. Christ also said this when he healed people: "This is because of my Father; I am only a channel."

A guru should receive your love and respect. If my guru and the Lord both come together, I will go to my guru first and say, "Thank you very much. You have introduced me to the Lord." I will not go to the Lord and say, "Thank you very much, Lord. You have given me my guru."

The master's ways of teaching are many and sometimes mysterious. He teaches through speech and actions, but in some cases he may teach without any verbal communication at all. The most important teachings have their source in intuition and are beyond the powers of verbal communication.

It is a great joy, perhaps the greatest day for a seeker, when she or he meets her/his beloved Master, who is totally selfless and loving like an ocean of bliss, overflowing with love all the time.

Search for the guru within yourself and anyone who leads you to your inner guru is your guru.

'Lotus feet' means the feet that are on the ground, but never touch the ground. One who lives in the world and does not belong to the world, one who is overflowing with love, for such a great soul the poets and writers say, 'lotus feet.'

Such a great man has power to show the path of freedom to others. Whether he is in the world or outside, he can also heal the sickness arising from karmic debts. He can remain untouched and above without being involved or reaping the fruits arising from others' karmic debts. A true master has control over himself and moves freely in the world.

When a potter has completed making his pots, the wheel of the potter still rotates for some time, but is unable to manufacture pots. For a liberated soul, the wheel of life remains in motion, but his karma does not create any bondage for him. His actions are called actionless actions. When the student is competent to tread the path of enlightenment, it becomes easy for a great man to guide him, and one day he also attains ultimate freedom.

Shaktipata

People think that by the grace of God alone they will be enlightened. That is not the case. My master said, "A human being should make all possible sincere efforts. When he has become exhausted, and then cries out in despair in the highest state of devotional emotion, he will attain ecstasy. That is the grace of God. Grace is the fruit that you receive from your faithful and sincere efforts."

Shaktipata is only possible with a disciple who has gone through a long period of discipline, austerity, and spiritual practices. Shaktipata on a mass scale seems suspicious to me. It is true that when the disciple is ready, the master appears and gives the appropriate initiation. When a student has done his sadhana with all faithfulness, truthfulness, and sincerity, then the subtlest obstacle is removed by the master. Those who do not believe in discipline should not expect enlightenment. No master can or will give it to them just because they want it.

The experience of enlightenment comes from the sincere effort of both master and disciple. Let us put it in different words. When you have done your duty skillfully and wholeheartedly, you reap the fruits gracefully. Grace dawns when action ends. Shaktipata is the grace of God through the master.

Silence

There was a swami who was considered to be a great adept, an accomplished one. His disciples went to him and said, "Sir, tell us something about the Ultimate Reality, or God." And he wouldn't say anything. He would smile but wouldn't say anything. He wouldn't reply anything. They became frustrated.

They said, "Sir, we have been constantly requesting you to tell us something about God, and you are simply smiling, you are not telling us anything."

You know what he said? He said, "I've been replying to you, but you are not listening to me."

And they said, "But you did not say a word!"

He said, "The best of the teachings are given in silence, so I am silently telling you."

So they said, "But we don't have the ear to hear. What did you tell, sir?"

He said, "God is silence."

Real knowledge, a practical knowledge, a deep, unspoken communication, and a teaching in silence pave their way beyond the mire of delusion.

The best of all knowledge, the greatest of all powers, comes from silence.

Reflections from the Silence

What I realize is that the life force is upon me
      to do what God wants,
      and not what I want.
No one will be able to rob this conviction of mine.
Many times I had the feeling that in all decisive matters
      I was no longer alone,
      I was beyond time.
      I felt that I was an ancient traveler,
      and belonged to the centuries.

The fierce loneliness of the blazing sun
      and utter annoyance of harsh winter
      were my companions.

Suddenly I get stunned
and go into silence.

I am one with the Supreme,
with the deathless,
with the Perfect.

Sometimes I feel with all my profundity
      as though a breath of the infinite world
      of stars and endless space
      has touched me.

When I bathe in sunlight
      with the winds and clouds
            moving over me,
      my experience becomes inexplicable.

I feel as though the sunshine recognizes me
        and with great delight
        I enjoy to sit under the shade of the moon.

When the sun goes to bed I remain awake.

It is a profound thought
        as though a breath of the infinite world
        of stars and endless space
        had touched me.

Yesterday evening I saw people bathing in sunlight
        with winds and clouds
                        running over them.

VIOLENCE

When for a moment I cast aside all rationalism
      and transport myself into the clear mountain air
      on the solitary rock,
      I spontaneously go into silence.

Solitude keeps me alive in a society
that knows no laws of love and harmony.

Violence, violence, violence
      everywhere.

I do not understand the law
that prompts mortal beings to injure each other.
How do they forget that all creatures are breathing
      one and the same breath?

Why are they ungrateful and why do they forget
      that all breathing beings
      are the children of one Father
      who is giving the life breath to all equally?

From where arises this violence?
Which is that power that instigates them
to annihilate each other's existence?

I return to my silence
      without any reply
      and with a simple conclusion
      that human beings have not yet really found out
      the art of living harmoniously.

The evil that forces one to commit such heinous crimes
        is because of *himsa*, the absence of love,
        consideration, kindness, and awareness
        that we all belong to One.

By killing others
        we are cutting the roots of the same tree
        whose limbs we are.

A THOUGHT

My religion knows neither hope nor fear.
It dwells in the calm of the spiritual universe
that nothing but the human heart can comprehend;
when the dew drop in the grass can mirror the heavens,
why not human mind and heart.

THE HOURS OF STILL NIGHT

With sovereign gesture you pour the content of your jug
        into my mouth, tempt me,
        and then disappear
        all of a sudden.

Out of this experience, unconscious content may arise,
        but I still feel thirsty.

You are acting like a living symbol of monstrosity.

I have climbed the highest of mountains
and searched the depth of the sea.

I have experienced that polarity
that is made up of two differentiated ideas,
have grown together,
and from one and the same source
springs the question
                why are you silent?

I suffer, for I am the victim.
I have a hope that one day
the merciful Lord will hasten to my aid.

When I begin to think in a clumsy way and decide
        that everything proceeds
        out of my intentions
        and out of myself,
        then my childlike naïve heart assumes
        that it knows all
        and knows what it is.

Yet all the while I am fatally handicapped
by the weakness of my conscious mind
and corresponding fear of the unconscious.

I am still thirsty.

This thirst leads me to that sort of dissatisfaction
in which I am always content,
but still unsatisfied.

I had a dream in my childhood that initiated me
        into the secrets of nature
        and I always loved to be a part of it.

Who says that a human being is an event
        that cannot judge itself but,
        better or worse,
        is left to the judgement of others?

I have seen people being humiliated
        in the eyes of the world,
        but elevated
        in the world of fantasy.

One should have the capacity to transport oneself
        into the mythic realm.
        Otherwise,
        the consequence is complete alienation
        from the world.

A DISTANT REALITY

Once I was talking to a friend of mine.
A strange feeling of fatefulness crept over me.
To my utter surprise
my friend was dwelling in a distant land of innocence
far away from reality
while I was plunged
into Reality.

The communication broke
and I found myself
      in a wide and silent emptiness of space.

It actually extended into isolated waste
from which sprang and sprawled
      a clumsy, tortured mass of dust.

AWAKENING

When I demanded clarity of mind,
mind was clouded and could not give it.
I could not destroy recklessly
the fireworks of my passions, lower mind.
I tried to hug all the worldly fetters.
Fate also was generous
to offer me all the possible gifts of life.

One day I woke up from the dream
  with the first ray of the sun
  with a feeling
  of having missed my future.

I tried to lift the veil of the future
and found out it is more hidden in the dream.

It is the realm of faith that creates perfection.

I have seen the records of the greatest dreamers
of the millennium,
but did not see love manifested in its beauty
in their teachings,
though they were designers of paradise.

Our physical life has its thread of unity
in the memory of the past,
whereas this ideal life dwells
in the prospective imagining
of the future.

From the buried records of the dust
I unearthed and found something flowing in me
  uninterrupted
    through the ages.

111

In order to give expression to it
I gathered the facts and found out
that I am not imperfect,
          but incomplete.

I know in myself some meaning is yet to be realized.
          It does not wonder me.
          I am just baffled.

I am a great dreamer
          who wants to reveal all his personalities
          in the service of humanity.

These expressions may not be holy
          but indirectly they belong to the image
          that is sealed silently
          in the inner chamber of my heart.

Today only I have come to a conclusion.
In this I find my own supreme value
          that I call divine.

Our dream in dark night ends thus
　　　　　　　on a sudden.

Truth shines forth
　　　and man says,
　　　　　"It is I."

Thus do scented flowers open up
　　　　　in the air,
　　　and a thousand rivers flow gently
　　　　　to the ocean.

HALLUCINATION OF A HERMIT

I remember it precisely.
One evening in the stillness of the night
I heard a voice saying, "I am with you."
I listened, fascinated.

It was not unusual for me
to tune into the chords of nature.
I started hearing soft music,
containing as well all the discords of nature.
Nature is not always harmonious;
she is also dreadfully contradictory and chaotic.

The music was that way too.
An outpouring of sound having the quality
of gushing rain and roaring wind—so impossible
that it is simply impossible to describe it.

It was late winter or late spring.
I gently opened my eyes and opened my window shutters.
There was no one in sight.

Nothing to be heard,
no wind,
nothing,
nothing at all.

This is strange I thought.
I was certain;
but apparently I had been daydreaming.

In the middle of this I fell asleep
and at once the same dream persisted.

At this point I woke up;
        same still night
        with a still moonlight.

For me this dream represented a situation equivalent to
reality, in which it created a kind of unknown state.

That night everything was so real,
I could scarcely sort out
the two realities.

A DREAM OF

Today is a tasteless day.
    A mysterious anguish of tired life
    lingers in my heart all the time.

Deep in the mountains far from human civilization,
    a single light that shines
    as night deepens
    I dream of.

A lovely flowery sentiment
    I dream of.

That light that shines in the sun, moon, and stars
    when night deepens
    I dream of.

Deep in the heart
    lonely and flowery feeling
    a mysterious anguish
    of a tired life's
    tasteless day.

I think of an unsolvable mystery.

I would like to steal that Love that gleams in the sky.

MY GURUDEVA

Thy memory has made a permanent abode
     in the inner chamber of my being
     and thy words
     are like the pouring of the pure spring
     of living water
     into the parched areas of my life.

From the far horizons of the world beyond
     often comes the calm voice
     reminding me
     that the inner spirit is the sole reality
     and that the fulfillment of this spirit
     is the secret of life.

Meditate, meditate, meditate.

A BLESSING

When I saw him first
I felt that a prophet of the Old Testament
had suddenly put on living flesh.
The silver white of his long hair and beard
melted into the white purity of his robe,
and in the dark,
his illuminated gentle face,
the eyes burned
with consciousness of power.

He spoke in a high delicate voice
      the words following one another
         like a flight of wild birds
            across a sunset sky.

He blessed me.

Next day in the hour of cowdust
I again visited a cave that has been my abode of peace.
I sat in a corner meditating
'til the full moon rose
and silvered the dark earth.

It shed its quiet radiance
peeping inside
and touched with new beauty
the finest head of Himalayas' outstanding sage
etching it there vividly
against the background of the Himalayan night.

He came from a glorious village of Bengal.
He refused to speak Bengali language.
For ten decades he breathed
the cloud kissed air of the Himalayas
and washed his body in the sacred river Ganges.

His touch revived the souls of many, many students.
The Vedas, Upanishads and Brahmins stood by him.

I knew my Master more
when he did not mutter a word,
surrounded by silence.
I could hear the voice of his thoughts,
singing to himself his own songs.

Flowers gathered from the valleys of the Himalayas,
　　　　and wealth brought from the mind trained in yogic
　　　　tradition, a difficult exploration of knowledge.

I do not totally believe in tradition.
In the process of growth I received experience.
Many times I found them alloyed
and sometimes unalloyed.
All my experiences do not guide me,
　　　　but a few experiences that I had,
　　　　not by the help of inheritance or importation,
　　　　but through vision,
　　　　are still my guide.

I have found the way of unlearning
　　　　all that I learned in my young age,
　　　　and also have the knowledge of recalling,
　　　　whenever I want,
　　　　the best I think I have stored
　　　　in my house of merits and demerits.

For nonyogis it can be considered a land of wisdom;
　　　　I feel it is not a stumbling block,
　　　　but helpful when I teach my students.

Those who dwell in a universe of history,
　　　　in an environment of continuous remembrance,
　　　　do not have the wisdom of living in the present.
How miserable are they!
Yogis have their special dwelling place
　　　　in the realm of inner realization.
This is a world of Reality—the subterranean soil
　　　　of deep consciousness.

All creative thoughts sprout here.
The luminous freedom is realized.
The underground current of this perennial stream
        vibrates the whole being.

I refused to persuade myself to accept
        the sayings of manmade religions.
I kept myself free from the influence and dominance
        of any creed that had its sanction in the rigid
        authority of some scriptures.
I always doubted the teaching of organized bodies of
        worshippers.

I also want to be questioned,
        and all have the right to distrust what I say;
        but, do not remain brooding,
        and at times do not forget to ask yourself,
        and learn to doubt your doubts too!

When I cast my eyes backward
        and find the voice ringing into my inner ear
        that you are on the right path,
        do I follow the blind path of obedience
        having rigidity of rules,
        or follow the voice that guides me?

The Upanishads are a great source of inspiration
        and solace to me.
They also say the same thing.

My knowledge is not through the mind.
It is through vision
　　　　that I receive in deep meditation
　　　　and contemplation.

Deep in the solitude and silence of dark night
      when the whole world remains asleep,
      I remain awake.

Now pour upon my brow
      the long sleep that knows no dreams.

O affectionate breath of the deep earth
      kiss me once again;
      let evening lapse into the silence.

Night drops its blossoms upon me
      and I spontaneously go into the silence
      that inspires my heart.

About the Author

Swami Rama was born in the Himalayas and was initiated by his master into many yogic practices. His master also sent Swamiji to other yogis and adepts of the Himalayas to gain new perspectives and insights into the ancient teachings. At the young age of twenty-four he was installed as Shankaracharya of Karvirpitham in South India. Swamiji relinquished this position to pursue intense sadhana in the caves of the Himalayas. Having successfully completed this sadhana, he was directed by his master to go to Japan and to the West in order to illustrate the scientific basis of the ancient yogic practices. At the Menninger Foundation in Topeka, Kansas, Swamiji convincingly demonstrated the capacity of the mind to control so-called involuntary physiological processes such as the heart rate, temperature, and brain waves. Swamiji's work in the United States continued for twenty-three years, and in this period he established the Himalayan International Institute of Yoga Science and Philosophy of the USA.

Swamiji became well known in the United States as a yogi, teacher, philosopher, poet, humanist, and philanthropist. His models of preventive medicine, holistic health, and stress management have permeated the mainstream of western medicine. In 1989 Swamiji returned to India where he established the Himalayan Institute Hospital Trust in the foothills of the Garhwal Himalayas.

Swamiji left this physical plane in November, 1996, but the seeds he has sown continue to sprout, bloom, and bear fruit. His teachings, embodied in the words, "Love, Serve, Remember," continue to inspire the many students whose good fortune it was to come in contact with such an accomplished, selfless, and loving master.

Himalayan Institute Hospital Trust

Perhaps the most visible form of Swami Rama's service to humanity is the Himalayan Institute Hospital Trust (HIHT). HIHT is a nonprofit organization committed to the premise that all human beings have the right to health, education, and economic self-sufficiency. The comprehensive health care and social development programs of HIHT incorporate medical care, education, and research. The philosophy of HIHT is: love, serve, remember.

The mission of the Trust is to develop integrated and cost-effective approaches to health care and development that address the local population, and which can serve as a model for the country as a whole, and for the underserved population worldwide. A combined approach in which traditional systems of health care complement modern medicine and advanced technology is the prime focus of clinical care, medical education, and research at HIHT.

HIHT is located in the newly formed state of Uttaranchal, one of the underdeveloped states of India. A bold vision to bring medical services to the millions of people in northern India, many of whom are underprivileged and have little or no health care, began modestly in 1989 with a small outpatient department. Today it is the site of a world class medical city and educational campus that includes: a large state-of-the-art hospital offering a full range of medical specialities and services, a holistic health program, a medical college, a school of nursing, a rural development institute, and accommodations for staff, students, and patients' families. This transformation is the result of the vision of Sri Swami Rama.

Himalayan Institute Hospital Trust
Swami Rama Nagar, P.O. Doiwala,
Distt. Dehradun 248140, Uttaranchal, India
Tel: 91-135-412068, Fax: 91-135-412008
hihtsrc@sancharnet.in; www.hihtindia.org